YOUR KNOWLEDGE HAS VALUE

Bibliographic information published by the German National Library:

The German National Library lists this publication in the National Bibliography;
detailed bibliographic data are available on the Internet at http://dnb.dnb.de .

Imprint:

Copyright © 2013 GRIN Verlag, Open Publishing GmbH
Print and binding: Books on Demand GmbH, Norderstedt Germany
ISBN: 9783656984375

This book at GRIN:

http://www.grin.com/en/e-book/333781/a-genetic-programming-approach-to-clas-
sification-problems

Hakan Uysal

A Genetic Programming Approach to Classification Problems

GRIN Publishing

GRIN - Your knowledge has value

Since its foundation in 1998, GRIN has specialized in publishing academic texts by students, college teachers and other academics as e-book and printed book. The website www.grin.com is an ideal platform for presenting term papers, final papers, scientific essays, dissertations and specialist books.

Visit us on the internet:

http://www.grin.com/

http://www.facebook.com/grincom

http://www.twitter.com/grin_com

A Genetic Programming Approach to Classification Problem

Hakan Uysal

Abstract

Genetic Programming is a biological evolution inspired technique for computer programs to solve problems automatically by evolving iteratively using a fitness function. The advantage of this type programming is that it only defines the basics. As a result of this, it is a flexible solution for broad range of domains. Classification has been one of the most compelling problems in machine learning. In this paper, there is a comparison between genetic programming classifier and conventional classification algorithms like Naive Bayes, C4.5 decision tree, Random Forest, Support Vector Machines and k-Nearest Neighbour. The experiment is done on several data sets with different sizes, feature sets and attribute properties. There is also an experiment on the time complexity of each classifier method.

1. Introduction

The world is going towards digitisation. Anything in the human life becomes data. Parallel to the improvement of the storage and database systems, storing the data and reaching to it have become easier and cheaper. However, having data does not mean knowledge. Information must be extracted from certain amount of the raw data. When it is done, the picture becomes clearer. This is where data mining starts.

Data mining[1] is the exploration and analysis of large quantities of data. Therefore extraction of interesting knowledge like patterns, rules or constraints from large data sets is essential.

Classification is the problem of identifying the categories of data. Text classification is one of the most idiosyncratic one among all. It is based on labelling the input text based on some training data. Social media and internet usage have been increasing by the acceptance of the real time communication and text based information sharing. Increasing amount of the text data boosts the importance of the knowledge extraction from this type. This leads computer science world to lean on text classification algorithms more. The most well known algorithms of this kind are decision tree, Naive-bayes, Random Forest, Support Vector Machines and K Nearest Neighbours classification.

Genetic programming, from then on GP, is a methodology which is inspired by biological evolution to solve computer related problems[10]. GP is a machine learning technique based on a fitness function which measures the performance of the given task. In the paper, GP is used to enhance the decision tree classification method to be able to classify text efficiently. After that the overall performance of this GP classifier is compared with the other popular classification algorithms.

1.1. Classification

Classification is categorisation process in which ideas and objects are understood and recognised. In statistics and data science, it is a problem of labelling data according to some training data. This operation is done by classifiers. One can say that classifiers are the learners from the training data and categorises the unlabelled input. Main purpose of the classification is making the predictor algorithm to learn the model of the data and start predicting based on this model.

1

Common method is that a data set is taken and it is divided into two parts. First part is training data which is used to train the classifier. Second part is called test data which is used to benchmark the performance of the classifier. The rationale is basic: teach learner something and give it some input to test what it learnt. However, there comes a couple of problems like overfitting and under-fitting. If the training data is not sufficient for the domain of the problem, under-fitting happens which is high bias to the data. On the other hand, if the training data is so complicated or big according to the domain of the problem and structure of the data set, overfitting happens which means high variance that causes the classifier can not limit to the possible scenarios due to the large space of hypothesis. These lead one to choose the training set and test set ratio neatly.

1.2. Decision Trees

Decision tree[2] is a learning method which is based on target functions with discrete values. Essentially, the model is created as a tree structure with nodes and leaves. Each node corresponds to a variable test and each leaf corresponds to a class label which is definitive of the decision made by classifier. This is a really popular algorithm to be used from finance to medicine.

Main purpose while creating a decision tree from a training data is to create the most compact decision tree possible. Because one can create multiple decision trees with the same training set. The key factor to set up a tree is the attribute selection for the internal nodes in order to create a compact tree. To standardize this process, 2 main methods can be used. These are information gain which calculates the knowledge stored in each training item's each attribute and gini index which is the measurement of the information distribution of attributes. There are a couple of well known algorithms to form up trees which are ID3, C4.5 and C5.0. In this experiment, J48 will be used to set up basic decision tree classifier. It's an open source Java implementation of C4.5 decision tree algorithm.

1.3. Naive-Bayes

Naive-Bayes is a classifier based on Bayes' theorem[3]. It's also known as independent feature model which comes from its naive acceptances. Naive-Bayesian classifier is widely used in pattern recognition field. Bayes' theorem:

$P(X)$: Probability of X $\qquad$ $P(X|Y)$: Probability of $X => Y$

$P(Y)$: Probability of Y $\qquad$ $P(Y|X)$: Probability of $Y => X$

1.4. Random Forest

Random forest is an algorithm which is simply based on creating a bulk of decision trees during runtime based on the random selection of features[4]. It's like an extension of decision tree classifier.

1.5. Support Vector Machines

Support Vector Machines, from then on SVM, is a learning and prediction method based on non probabilistic binary linear classification[6]. Basically SVM takes the patterns which are linearly separable and moves them into a hyperplane space. The patterns which are not linearly separable are transformed into new space and mapped with original data by using some kernel function. If there is no kernel function used, it means it is linear SVM, which is the most basic method.

The advantage of SVM is that it is a theoretical model of learning and its performance is guaranteed in theory. It also has a modular design which gives the one to add/ remove components.

SVM is one of the essential algorithms of pattern recognition. In this experiment, multi class SVM learner is also used for some of the data sets which have a number of class labels more than 2. To achieve this, each categorical input variable is converted into an indicator variable and for N multi-class problem, multiple binary classifiers are built for the operation.

2

1.6.K Nearest Neighbours

K Nearest Neighbours, from then on kNN, is an instance-based classification algorithm where the function is created locally and all of the computation is postponed until classification[5]. In simple words, whole training data set is loaded into the classifier and whenever a new test data comes, the distance of this test item to the each training item is calculated and test item is labeled as the nearest training item's class. More advanced method is that instead of simple distance calculation to each training data, certain number of nearest neighbours are checked and the label with the most number of items is used for classifying that test item. kNN gives very effective results in the field of image processing. IBk is an implementation of a classifier using kNN as search algorithm.

1.7.Genetic Algorithm

Genetic Algorithm, shortly GA, is a probabilistic search method which is based on converting a population of binary strings which have fixed lengths iteratively into a new population of offspring objects using an evolutionary principle. This supports crossover and mutation. It uses a fitness function to measure the success of population in order to get better candidates for the next iteration. This is inspired by natural selection. Steps of genetic algorithms are listed:

```
evaluate_fitness():                         1.   initialize_population()
        if end_condition:                   2.   evaluate_fitness()
                End                         3.   if is_population_full:
        else:                                        evaluate_fitness()
                start_new_population()      4.   else:
                                                     mutate(), copy(),
                                                     crossover()
                                                     population.add(offsprng)
                                                     goto 3
```

Crossover and mutation are totally random phases of this method.

1.8.Genetic Programming

Genetic programming, shortly GP, is an outgrowth of genetic algorithms. GP uses biological evolution as inspiration to perform artificial intelligence tasks[9]. GP's most important part is its fitness function. Basically it measures how well the task is performed by the algorithm. It helps the algorithm to get better and interestingly it can simply be similar to the natural selection in biology.

GP is widely used for optimisation problems by defining fitness functions for that specific problem.GP adopts almost everything from GA. However, during the mutation and crossover, instead of binary strings, programs are used.

GP is used to optimise the creation of the decision tree in this experiment. As mentioned above, compactness is the biggest challenge during the setup of a decision tree. An

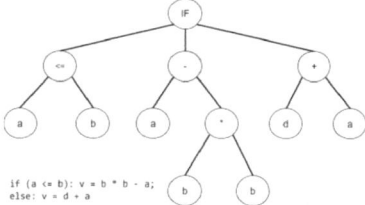

evolutionary method proves that GP is a good use case for classification problems[10].

Figure 1: Example tree representation of a GP

2. Experiment

This paper is based on experimenting different text classification algorithms and comparing their performance on a common and fair ground. To achieve this, 3 different data sets are chosen. They have different numbers of data rows. Therefore, the impact of the data set can be seen by checking their performance. In addition to this, the effect of the nominal and numerical features is also observed in case GP can outperform the conventional classification algorithms .

The purpose of this experiment is to understand which text classification algorithm performs better in terms of time and accuracy under different circumstances. Because as it's known, there is no perfect classifier which has high accuracy in every condition.

2.2. Data Sets

Data sets are all taken from UCI machine learning repository.

Name	Labels	Instances	Attrs	Missing?	Type
adult	Bivariate	48842	14	yes	categorical, int
breast cancer	Multi	699	10	no	categorical
car	Multi	1728	6	no	categorical
iris	Multi	150	4	no	real
contact-lenses	Multi	24	4	no	categorical
labor	Multi	57	16	no	categorical, int, real
segment-challenge	Multi	2310	19	no	real
soybean	Multi	307	35	no	categorical, int
weather	Bivariate	14	5	no	categorical
weather.nom	Bivariate	14	5	no	categorical

Table 1: Data set structures

2.3. Tools and Frameworks

Here are the tools used in this experiment[7].

Weka: It's an open source Java data mining and machine learning tool developed by University of Waikato, New Zealand. In the experiment, its Java API is heavily used to create classifiers and evaluate the results. Its GUI is used for sanity checks mostly[8].

Rapidminer: This is a full featured open source data mining tool. This is used for sanity checks for conventional machine learning classifiers like the ones listed at 2.4.

Orange: This is a Python and Qt based, simple UI machine learning tool. It does not allow high level of customisation. However, it has a powerful python API to automate processes. It's used for comparing results with weka API's time complexity performance.

2.4. Compared Algorithms

C4.5 Decision tree	Naive Bayes	Support Vector Machines
Random Forest	K Nearest Neighbour	GP Classifier

2.5. Genetic Programming Classifier

GP classifier is an optimised decision tree based algorithm which is supposed to create more compact trees[12].

In smartphone usage example, the class labels are "Yes" and "No" which are decisions taken at the end. We applied the same approach to the data sets given at 2.1. The programming structure has a population of decision trees[13]. Purpose of the GP here is that finding the best fitted decision tree for the problem and try to predict the test data. A fitness function which is explained at 2.6 is used to achieve this. Trees is not necessarily symmetric or full. There are 2 types of nodes in each tree, first of whom is the internal node which has 2 descendants and second of whom is the class label node. Initialisation of the population is done by ramping half and half method[11]. As stated at 1.7th section, Mutation whose aim is to generate diverse populations is applied on the 2 properties of the decision trees. Firs aspect is about the shape and height of the tree and the second one is the information held in each node. If more informative ones stored in the nodes which are close to the root, the classification finishes faster, tree becomes more compact, accuracy increases. The approach for the second one is using a replacement of a random node with a new random subtree. The

4

chance of mutation of each tree is around 25%. The next step is the mutation which aims to combine best performing nodes in tree. Selection phase is deterministic and simple. Both parents and children are removed from the population and after crossover and mutation, the fittest ones are added back[11]. There is also elite population kept in the memory whose experimented sizes are 5, 10, 15. 5 and 10 are experimented as maximum depth of each candidate tree. The population sizes observed are 50, 100 and 200.

2.6. Evaluation

10-fold cross validation method is used to evaluate the performances of each learner. Main evaluation criterions are listed:

Precision: Ratio of relevant and irrelevant results.

Recall: How many of the relevant results are retrieved.

ROC (AUC): Area under curve. Although data sets vary in terms of structure and size, ROC area usually gives the best idea of how successful the classifier is.

Accuracy: This is the distance of the predicted values to reference values.

TP Rate: True positive rate which means how many of the test data is classified correctly. True negative or false positive or false negative rate can also be used here. However, preferably, TP rate is the most human readable and meaningful one.

The selected fitness function in the experiment is the TP rate whose formula is:

```
tpRate = (#correctly classified items) / (#population) * 100
```

Considering the randomness element of the GP, for each data set, validator is run on each classifier. 10 times and the results with the highest AUC value is taken into the report.

3. Results

3.1. Accuracy

The key success metric in this experiment is the true positive rate, ROC area precision and recall. They altogether define the accuracy of the classifier. The bigger elite size brought the higher true positive rates. Increasing elite size from 5 to 10, boosted the TP rate around 9.75% in average which is pretty significant value. The bigger elite size brought the higher true positive rates. Increasing elite size from 5 to 10, boosted the TP rate around 9.75% in average which is pretty significant value. Full analysis and raw data is available[16].

3.1.1. Adult Data Set

Classifier	Attrs	AUC	Precision	Recall	TpRate
J48	15	89.15%	85.70%	86.23%	86.23%
RandomForest	15	87.65%	83.44%	84.13%	84.13%
NaiveBayes	15	89.21%	82.47%	83.43%	83.43%
IBk	15	71.50%	79.26%	79.42%	79.42%
SVM	15	50.11%	70.51%	75.93%	75.93%
GP	15	67.00%	80.21%	81.51%	81.51%

Table 2: Adult data set classification accuracy

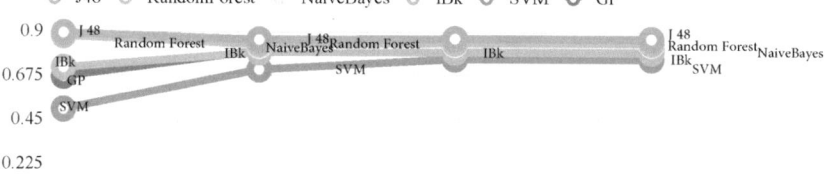

Figure 2: Adult data set classification performance

5

Adult data set is the biggest data set experimented in this paper. As it can be seen, it's multi class structure makes the predictions less successful in SVM. Because by nature, SVM is a bi-class learning method. GP performed close to IBk and the other ones. Considering that there are 48842 instances and 15 attributes, the search space for GP will be really high, nevertheless it's still successful.

3.1.2.Breast Cancer Wisconsin Data Set

Classifier	Attrs	AUC	Precision	Recall	TpRate
J48	10	95.47%	94.58%	94.56%	94.56%
RandomForest	10	99.01%	95.71%	95.71%	95.71%
NaiveBayes	10	98.60%	96.16%	95.99%	95.99%
IBk	10	97.31%	95.12%	95.14%	95.14%
SVM	10	96.75%	96.32%	95.99%	95.99%
GP	10	94.74%	95.55%	95.55%	95.56%

Table 3: Breast cancer data set classification accuracy

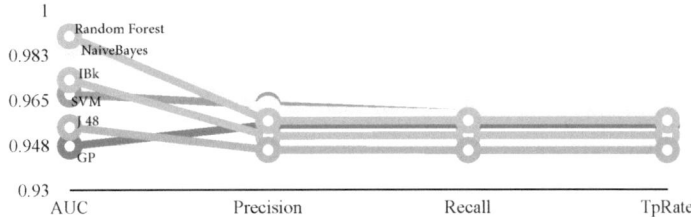

Figure 3: Breast cancer data set classification performance

This is a medium size data set with 699 instances with 10 attributes. It's a pretty decent data set to measure the classification performance. Because the class labels are distributed uniformly. As it can be seen from the TP rate, all of the classifiers performing almost same. Precision and recall values are also close. GP became successful at this one.

3.1.3.Car Data Set

Classifier	Attrs	AUC	Precision	Recall	TpRate
J48	7	97.64%	92.43%	92.36%	92.36%
RandomForest	7	98.83%	93.10%	93.06%	93.06%
NaiveBayes	7	97.56%	85.19%	85.53%	85.53%
IBk	7	99.70%	94.03%	93.52%	93.52%
SVM	7	97.03%	96.42%	96.35%	96.35%
GP	7	76.09%	78.52%	80.09%	80.09%

Table 4: Adult data set classification accuracy

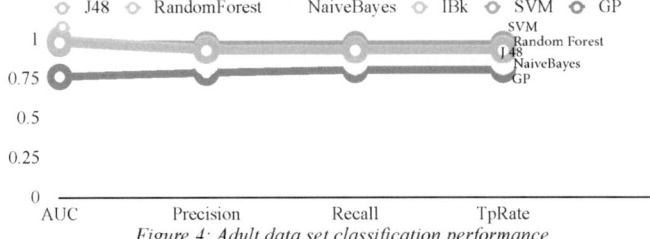

Figure 4: Adult data set classification performance

Results of Car data set are put on purpose to show the weak points of GP classifier. Although it is a fairly big data set, it is multi class and class labels are not distributed uniformly. It is one of the weakest points of this GP classifier. It's not so immune to the data set and its performance is struck by the form of the structure.

3.1.4.Iris Data Set

Classifier	Attrs	AUC	Precision	Recall	TpRate
J48	5	96.76%	96.04%	96.00%	96.00%
RandomForest	5	98.05%	94.01%	94.00%	94.00%
NaiveBayes	5	99.44%	96.05%	96.00%	96.00%
IBk	5	96.63%	95.34%	95.33%	95.33%
SVM	5	97.50%	96.68%	96.67%	96.67%
GP	5	97.50%	96.68%	96.67%	96.67%

Table 5: Iris data set classification accuracy

Figure 5: Iris data set classification performance

This is the most common data set in machine learning with 3 uniformly distributed class labels. As stated before, GP classifier works well on this type of sets. So GP got the highest TP rates among all classifiers. In the chart it's almost same as SVM.

3.1.5.Contact Lenses Data Set

Classifier	Attrs	AUC	Precision	Recall	TpRate
J48	5	83.97%	85.05%	83.33%	83.33%
RandomForest	5	89.14%	72.92%	75.00%	75.00%
NaiveBayes	5	87.01%	69.10%	70.83%	70.83%
IBk	5	91.39%	80.24%	79.17%	79.17%
SVM	5	47.37%	38.04%	58.33%	58.33%
GP	5	75.70%	75.62%	75.00%	75.00%

Table 6: Contact lenses data set classification accuracy

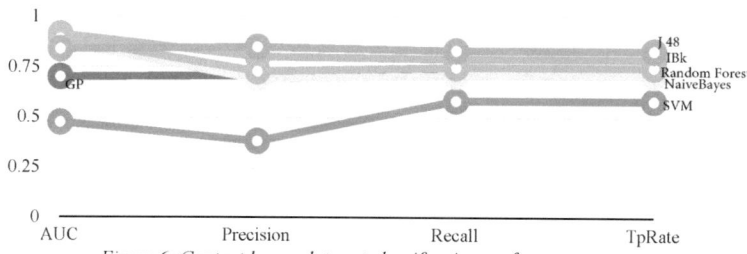

Figure 6: Contact lenses data set classification performance

This data set is tricky because it is fairly small 24 instances and it has 3 class labels with non-uniform distribution. TP Rate of all of the classifiers went down due to the lack of training set. GP's performance was not the worst. This data set is also a success for GP.

3.1.6.Soybean Data Set

Classifier	Attrs	AUC	Precision	Recall	TpRate
J48	36	98.34%	91.65%	91.51%	91.51%
RandomForest	36	99.24%	92.96%	92.53%	92.53%
NaiveBayes	36	99.45%	93.83%	92.97%	92.97%
IBk	36	97.51%	91.52%	91.22%	91.22%
SVM	36	96.51%	94.64%	93.85%	93.85%
GP	36	50.74%	9.56%	4.98%	4.98%

Table 7: Soybean data set classification accuracy

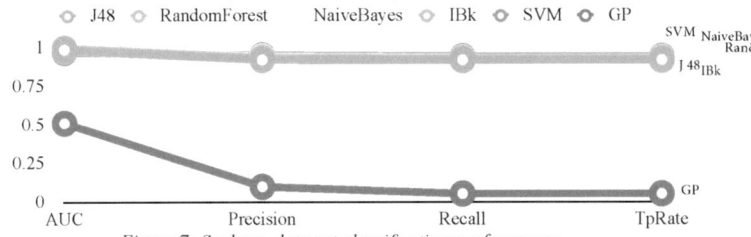

Figure 7: Soybean data set classification performance

Soybean data set is another famous one with 683 instances with 19 class labels. This is a characteristic example to understand the weak points of the GP. The class labels are not distributed uniformly. 19 class labels with 36 attributes cause a lot of branching in the decision tree. This does not necessarily mean a bad thing. However, GP generates certain number of population which is formed by decision trees. This causes a giant search space so missing valuable nodes during crossover and mutation becomes more probable. As a result of this most of the test data is classified wrong. ~5% is really unsuccessful.

3.1.7.Weather Nominal Data Set

Classifier	Attrs	AUC	Precision	Recall	TpRate
J48	5	63.33%	52.08%	50.00%	50.00%
RandomForest	5	55.56%	52.81%	57.14%	57.14%
NaiveBayes	5	57.78%	52.81%	57.14%	57.14%
IBk	5	48.41%	57.14%	57.14%	57.14%
SVM	5	50.00%	41.33%	64.29%	64.29%
GP	5	73.33%	75.51%	71.42%	71.42%

Table 8: Weather data set classification accuracy

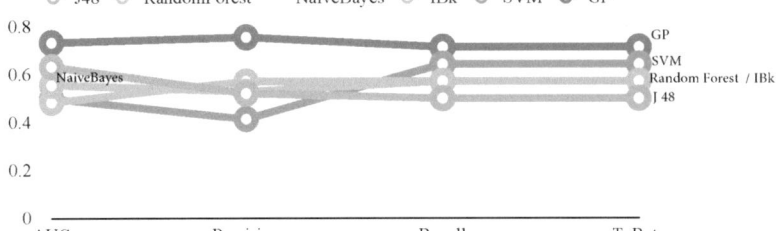

Figure 8: Contact lenses data set classification performance

Weather data set is a symbolic one with 14 instances with 5 attributes. It's fairly uniformly distributed 2 class labels. As it can be seen from the chart, GP is the most successful one. This also approves the statements given for the other data sets. GP does well with fewer and uniformly distributed class labels. The other classifiers did not have enough training data to generate their models.

3.2. Time Complexity Comparison (seconds)

Dataset	Size	J48	RandFores	NaiveBays	IBk	SVM	GP
adult	48842	14.281	32.400	0.704	64.954	4321.269	147.210
Breast-cancer	699	0.088	0.167	0.020	0.054	0.266	19.645
car	1728	0.035	0.248	0.015	0.152	0.938	24.296
iris	150	0.007	0.030	0.004	0.007	0.016	7.291
Contact-lenses	24	0.004	0.012	0.003	0.004	0.004	1.177
labor	57	0.007	0.056	0.004	0.006	0.012	1.706
Segment	2310	0.340	0.795	0.083	0.131	4.379	27.684
soybean	307	0.074	0.551	0.034	0.081	0.644	22.790
weather	14	0.004	0.010	0.002	0.004	0.002	0.666
weather.nom	14	14.281	32.400	0.704	64.954	4321.269	147.210

Table 9: Average time elapsed after 10 times of running

Genetic Programming is a computational heavy and some kind of a brute force technique to solve the problems. Since it's inspired by the biological evolution which obviously takes time, GP solutions also take time. However, according to the environment of the problem, time complexity might not be the key metric. In most of the problems classification quality comes before timing.

As it can be seen in the table, apart from SVM, the conventional algorithms, J48, Random Forest, Naive Bayes and IBk take less than a second in most cases. Even the biggest data set which is the adult one with 48k rows took 2 seconds in average. Support Vector Machines are used for mostly learning. So building the classifier in the beginning takes a significant amount of time. Therefore doing a 10 fold cross validation also takes huge amount of time. IBk is not learning so it's always fast regardless of the data size. J48 and Random Forest spend some time on setting up trees. So they fall behind Naive Bayes and IBk.

Other parameters are also used; increasing the elite population size gave us more true positive rate. However, it brought the time complexity up around 20% in average. There observed an increase while using bigger population sizes in GP classifier which was expected. Because search space gets broader.

4. Conclusion

Experiment has shown that classification still stays as a hard problem to solve. However, genetic programming has brought a couple of new tools on the table which have a lot of room for further development and optimisation due to GP's short history. The more work done on GP, the more optimised results you get. The rationale under this is that GP has lots of parameters to consider while solving a classification problem. Initial population, population size, tree heights, fitness function, crossover rate, mutation rate, crossover function, mutation function, selection logic, target fitness, elite population size, preprocessing. GP has also element of surprise which is the randomness. It's both good and bad. Because it increases the diversity and combines valuable nodes together, but it also makes tracking of the performance harder. If you run Naive Bayes classifier 100 times, the TP rates will be almost typical. However, if you run GP classifier 100 times, it's highly likely to see some significant changes in the results. To come over this, GP classifier is run several times and got the best result out of those experiments.

Disadvantages of GP classifier are needing fine tunes for parameters, being vulnerable to the unstructured data sets with non-uniform distributions, taking time to finish, having randomness in the results.

To sum up, GP is a very promising field for addressing classification problems. Developing more libraries, frameworks and tools can make significant changes in the understanding of machine learning. Currently, although there are handful of data mining tools, there is no decent GP classifier in them.

5. Future Work

Importance of GP has been increasing more and more every day. It's a niche field which is open for development. There are a couple of future researches. First one is comparing the performance of GP and Artificial Neural networks[15] which is another Natural computing algorithm based on the biological neural nets. Second one is to use some data preprocessing before running the classifier to clean up the data. It's possible to get better results from the GP classifier by using this method. Feature selection will be another part of this future study as well. Using a ranker algorithm to select the N attributes with the most information gain might be a good way to boost the performance of GP classifier.

Another aspect of development is the upturning of search space. Because during the classification the boundaries are so vague and hard to anticipate. It makes search space fairly large. In that case, an optimisation like parallelism or partitioning could be useful[14].

Development of an open source python GP classifier for Orange data mining tool is also in the roadmap.

References

1. Fayyad, Usama; Piatetsky-Shapiro, Gregory; Smyth, Padhraic (1996). "From Data Mining to Knowledge Discovery in Databases". Retrieved 17 December 2008.
2. Y. Yuan and M.J. Shaw, Induction of fuzzy decision trees. Fuzzy Sets and Systems 69 (1995), pp. 125–139
3. McCallum, Andrew, and Kamal Nigam. "A comparison of event models for Naive Bayes text classification." AAAI-98 workshop on learning for text categorization. Vol. 752. 1998.
4. Breiman, Leo (2001). "Random Forests". Machine Learning 45 (1): 5–32. doi:10.1023/A:1010933404324
5. Cover TM, Hart PE (1967). "Nearest neighbor pattern classification". IEEE Transactions on Information Theory 13 (1): 21–27. doi:10.1109/TIT.1967.1053964.
6. Cortes, Corinna; and Vapnik, Vladimir N.; "Support-Vector Networks", Machine Learning, 20, 1995.
7. Informatics Research and Development Unit, Open Source Data Mining Software Evaluation, 2010 report.
8. A Tool for Model Generation and Knowledge Acquisition (1993), Sally Jo Cunningham, Paul Denize
9. Koza, J.R. (1992), Genetic Programming: On the Programming of Computers by Means of Natural Selection, MIT Press
10. Koza, J.R. (1994), Genetic Programming II: Automatic Discovery of Reusable Programs, MIT Press
11. Banzhaf, W., Nordin, P., Keller, R.E., Francone, F.D. (1998), Genetic Programming: An Introduction: On the Automatic Evolution of Computer Programs and Its Applications, Morgan Kaufmann
12. Representing classification problems in genetic programming (2001), Loveard, T. ; Dept. of Comput. Sci., R. Melbourne Inst. of Technol., Vic., Australia ; Ciesielski, V.
13. Algorithme De Pg, Tiré Du Mémoire Techniques De L'intelligence Artificielle Pour La Reconnaissance D'objets Biologiques Dans Une Image (2008), Yan Par Levasseur
14. Genetic Programming for Data Classification: Partitioning the Search Space (2004), Jeroen Eggermont, Joost N. Kok, Walter A. Kosters
15. Ferreira, C. (2006). "Designing Neural Networks Using Gene Expression Programming". In A. Abraham, B. de Baets, M. Köppen, and B. Nickolay, eds., Applied Soft Computing Technologies: The Challenge of Complexity, pages 517–536, Springer-Verlag
16. Source code and full analysis results: https://github.com/hakanu/weka-gp-classifier